A story by Lori Henninger Smith

Finn's Friend Fungie

Fungie the dolphin famous in Dingle Bay,

has just up and gone away.

Illustrations by Alice Pescarin

ISBN: 978-1-7379407-1-5

Finn's Friend Fungie
Library of Congress Control Number: 2021923191

Silver Girl Sails Publishing, Ltd.
Little Rock, AR USA

Copyright © 2021
A story by Lori Henninger Smith
Illustrations by Alice Pescarin

www.finnandfungiebooks.com

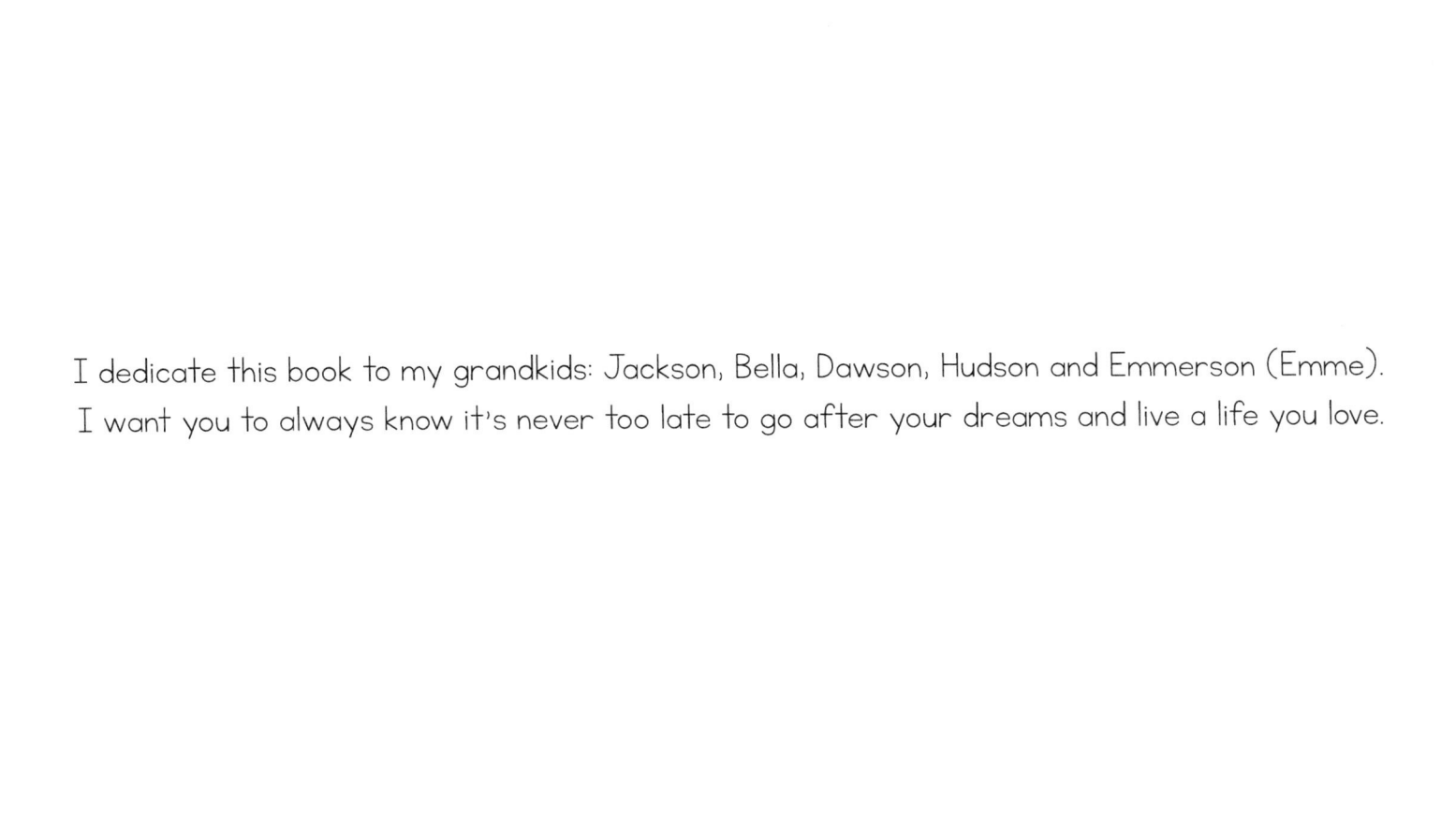

I dedicate this book to my grandkids: Jackson, Bella, Dawson, Hudson and Emmerson (Emme). I want you to always know it's never too late to go after your dreams and live a life you love.

TO BEGIN LISTENING TO THIS BOOK, SCAN THIS CODE. TURN THE PAGE WHEN YOU HEAR THE DOLPHIN SQUEAK! HAVE FUN!

SCAN AND LISTEN

Little **dolphin,** where did you **go?**

We've been searching **high and low.**

Don't you know that **we miss you so?**

Finn has a friend named Fungie, did you know?
Finn's friend Fungie put on quite the show.

SCAN AND LEARN

In a town called **Dingle**, Fungie was a star!
And now he has run off, but how far?

How far did Finn's friend Fungie travel? **Oh my!**
The town misses him so much, and they want to know why!

Just as Finn was discovered in Carlingford Lough,
the people of Dingle began to talk.

Why did our dolphin
we've had for over thirty years,
become the dolphin who just disappeared?

Fungie was his name and he was loved by so many.
All of Ireland wanted to find a reason he left, **if any.**

SCAN AND LEARN

No one knew where he went or how long he'd be gone.
But they sure hoped they'd hear from him before too long.

Some kids said "Let's ask Finn, the dolphin of Carlingford Lough."
Perhaps he knew the answer, or perhaps not.

Finn started to squeak and squeal and got carried away,
wanting to tell us the story of his friend, Fungie, in Dingle Bay.
He began his story in dolphin speak and for anyone listening,
that sure is a treat!

Finn wanted to start with some history about his friend Fungie, so everyone will know how he filled the town with glee.

SCAN AND LEARN

He began with no one knows exactly what happened that day.
The day Finn's friend Fungie arrived in Dingle Bay.

Over thirty years ago, an even number, not odd,
a young dolphin got separated from his family pod...

That is what Dolphins normally swim in, a large group of dolphins, **it provides protection.**

Being a young dolphin, it was easy to **get distracted.**
He saw pretty boats and people, and to them he was attracted.

SCAN AND LEARN

SCAN AND LEARN

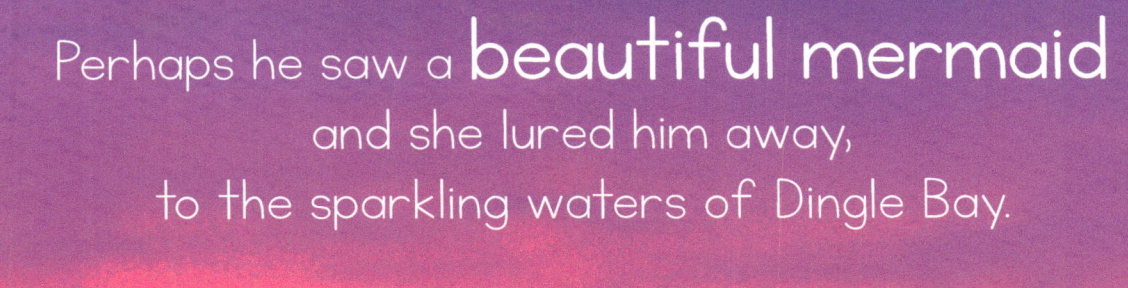

Perhaps he saw a **beautiful mermaid**
and she lured him away,
to the sparkling waters of Dingle Bay.

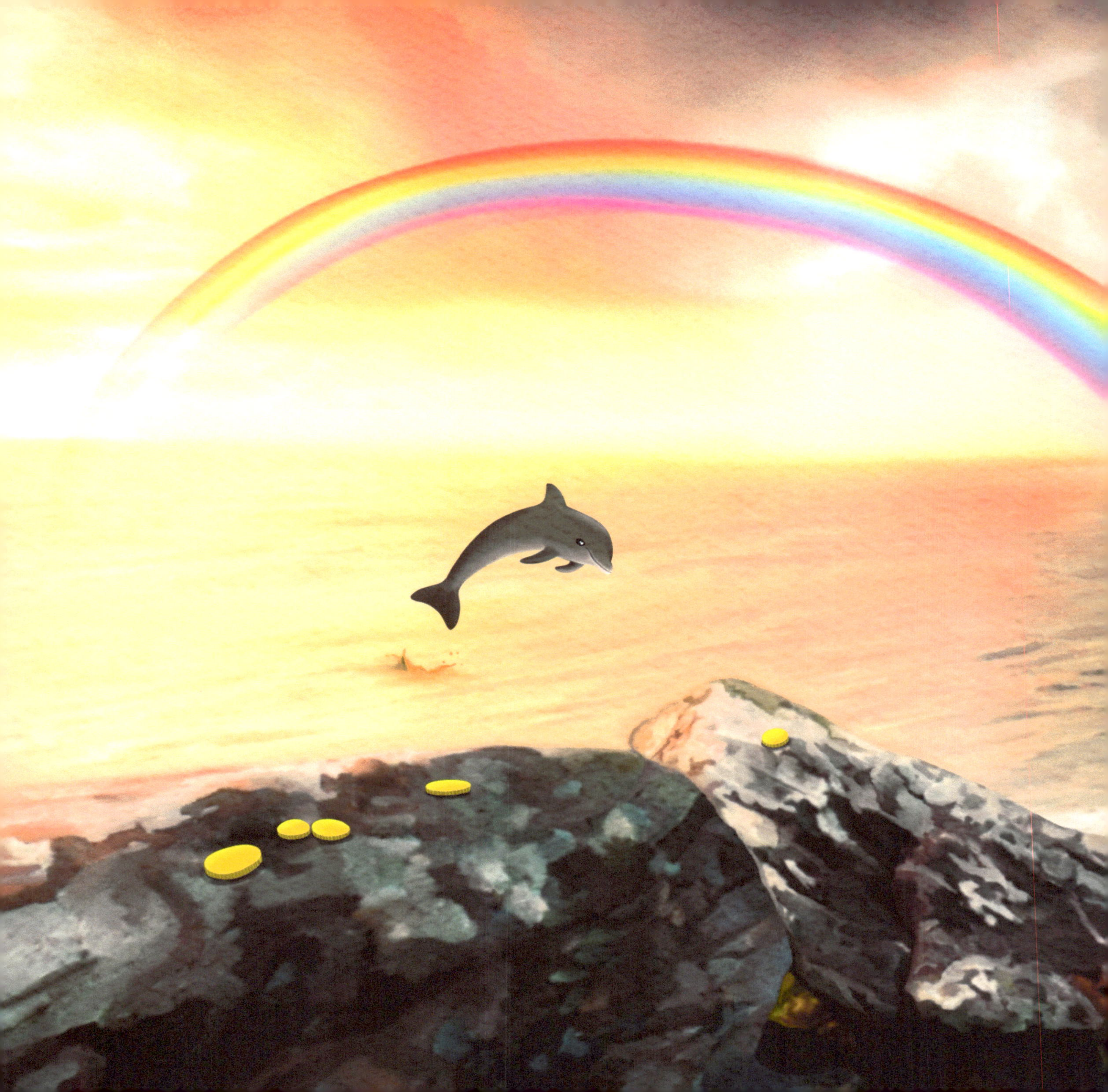

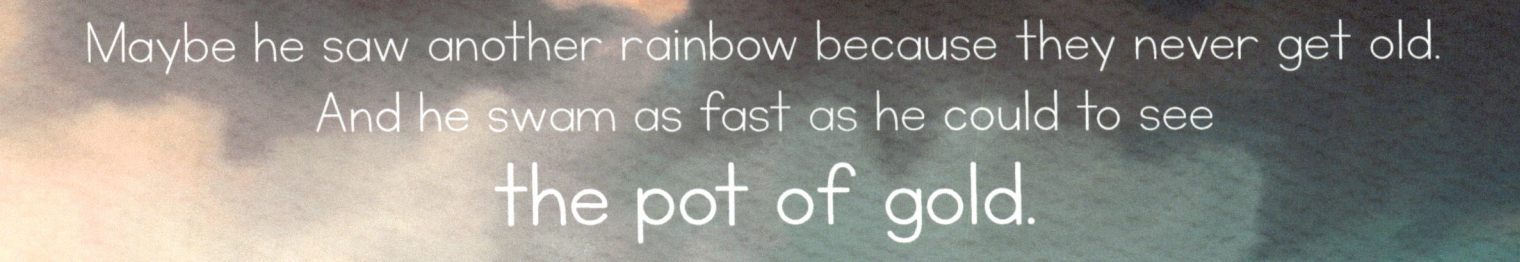

Maybe he saw another rainbow because they never get old.
And he swam as fast as he could to see
the pot of gold.

Well, as rainbows do, it disappeared
before he found the end,
but in the meantime he found a new friend.

SCAN AND LEARN

A fisherman named **Paddy** became his fast friend, coming out daily to check on him.

SCAN AND LEARN

Fungie began escorting fishing boats in and out of the bay.
He was given the title **Boat Pilot** one day.

For decades he swam,
jumped and splashed around, delighting anyone that he found.

But after many years, he decided it was time to go.
And he asked his friend Finn to let everyone know.

SCAN AND LEARN

He was happy in Dingle and will always remember the town,
who had rallied around him and never let him down.

He wants to explore the world and visit family and friends.
He wants to travel and learn about other cultures and trends.

He heard you can learn so much by expanding your universe. You just have to be brave enough to want it first.

Finn's friend Fungie stopped by on his travels to play.
Some kids saw him out there one day.

Did you see him playing **down by the shore?**
Splashing around by the ferry boat in Greenore?

Keep a look out for him, too,
because instead of one dolphin in Carlingford Lough,

maybe there's two?

SCAN AND LEARN

He told his friend Finn of his plans for **new adventures** and he set off with cheer.

Golden Gate Bridge, San Francisco, USA

Maybe he'll be back **to say hi** before the next thirty years.

Whether that's true or not,

we'll never know, but

Eiffel Tower, Paris, France

dolphins
are happy wherever they go.

SCAN AND LEARN

Finn's friend Fungie
we hope you do well...

Love,
Fungie

Sydney Opera House, Sydney, Australia

and come back from your travels
with lots of stories to tell.

SCAN AND LEARN

We miss you Fungie

with all of our hearts,
and hope to see you again soon around these parts....

Wherever you are,
we know you're filling everyone with glee...

that's just who you are,
Finn's friend Fungie!

Meet the real Fungie

Fungie arrived in Dingle in 1983. Some think he was already about 9-10 years old at that time. He captured the hearts and minds of Ireland and the whole world alike for almost four decades.

A Facebook page dedicated to the most famous, beloved dolphin in the world belongs to Fungie. It's called Fungie Forever – Photos of the Dingle Dolphin.
Here's the link.
https://www.facebook.com/12FungieForever12

Photographers Jeannine Masset and her husband Rudi Schamhart had the amazing opportunity of being around Fungie for decades. Can you just imagine that?
Getting to live life with an amazing dolphin that became part of your family?

They are amazing photographers. Fungie was amazing. And through the eyes of Jeannine and Rudi, Fungie will live on forever.

Check out our website for more fun information on Fungie!
www.finnandfungiebooks.com

Photos by Jeannine Masset

The person credited with first spotting the lone, playful dolphin in the sparkling waters of Dingle Bay was Dingle Harbour Lighthouseperson, Paddy Ferriter. Paddy was known for preferring the company of other species to his own kind, and it looks like Fungie felt that way, too. Both loners who found each other, and created a long friendship that stood the test of time.

Did you know Fungie was named after him? Paddy was teased by his friends, about his beard being scruffy and looked like a fungus on his face. Fungie got his name from that term of endearment.

In September of 2019, Fungie was entered into the Guinness Book of World Records for being the longest lived solitary dolphin. For over 37 years, Fungie graced the harbour of Dingle Bay and the town will remember him fondly forever.

Paddy Ferriter
photo by Seán Ó Mainnín

of Dingle Bay!

Did YOU know?

Did you know this book turns into an audio book by scanning the code on the dedication page? You can listen as Irish Folksinger Orla Travers narrates the book for you! That's fun when you're tired and still want to hear a story at bedtime!

Did you know you can scan these codes through-out the books to learn more about dolphins or castles or other things in the book? And those lessons will change from time to time! So next time, you may learn something new!

Did you know you are helping to free whales and dolphins around the world by reading this book? A portion of all proceeds goes to Marine Connection to help captive whales and dolphins retire to seaside sanctuaries. www.marineconnection.org

Did you know we have a website with fun stuff to do? You can get colouring sheets, and lesson plans for teachers and watch videos of Finn and Fungie and much more! Be sure to check it out!

www.finnandfungiebooks.com

Did you know you can help us tell other people about the books by writing a review on Amazon? Your review will help us raise money for Marine Connection to help more dolphins! Be sure to go to Amazon to write a review! We appreciate it so much!

Finn and Fungie want to thank you for helping them help other dolphins and whales live freely as they are meant to! They are so happy to have you on their team!

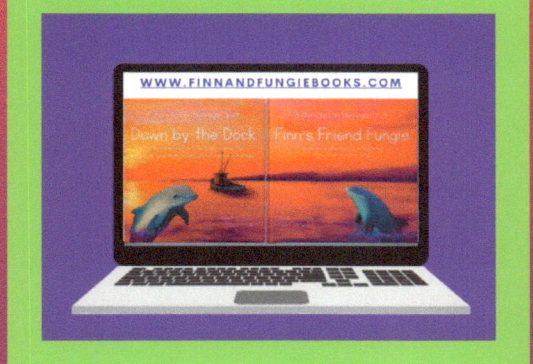

Thank you for your review!

Thank you Carlingford and Dingle and all of Ireland and the world! We love you, too! Signed, Finn and Fungie

About these **fun** things?

Meet the Author

Lori Henninger Smith

I studied studio art and graphic design at the University of Arkansas at Little Rock, USA. After a long career in marketing and home decor product design, I crossed the Atlantic Ocean to return to college at the age of 57.

Always in love with Ireland, I chose to study Public Relations and Digital Marketing Communications. With the encouragement of my creative writing lecturer, Ciara, I found my purpose. From my home on the waters of Carlingford Lough, (pronounced 'lock' for my American friends), I heard stories of a curious new and rare, dolphin in the area and began to imagine where this dolphin came from. Always enthralled by the folklore, myths and legends in Ireland that include giants, I could imagine a story evolving I knew my grandkids would enjoy. And "Down by the Dock" was born.

Then a friend mentioned the story of Fungie and after much research, "Finn's Friend Fungie" became a reality as well. Both books have been well received and we hope you enjoy them, too!

Thank you, Finn and Fungie, for helping me discover my passion.